Coding is Fun!

Eugene Amadi

Torchflame Books

Durham, NC

Copyright © Eugene Amadi 2019

Coding is Fun
Eugene Amadi
www.bugzero.codes
eugene@bugzero.codes

Published 2019, by Torchflame Books
  an Imprint of Light Messages Publishing
www.lightmessages.com
Durham, NC 27713 USA
SAN: 920-9298

ISBN: 978-1-61153-349-1

Trademarks: Bugzero.codes™ and the Bugzero.codes™ logo are trademarks of Bugzero.codes

Illustrations by Taimy Studio

Reserved Rights: No part of this publication may be reproduced, stored in a retrieval system, or transmitted in any form or by any means, electronic, mechanical, photocopying, recording, scanning, or otherwise, except as permitted under Section 107 or 108 of the 1976 International Copyright Act, without the prior written permission except in brief quotations embodied in critical articles and reviews.

Coding is used to program robots.

Video Games use code.

Transportation apps use code to show where you are and help you go where you want to go.

Everyday appliances use code. Even a washing machine uses code to know what cycle to use.

Coding is used to forecast the weather.

Online shopping uses code to prepare and ship orders.

Medical technology uses coding to help doctors with research and treatment.

Remote controls use code to make toys move.

You can watch a movie on your computer because of code.

Elevators are coded to know if they need to go up or down and when to stop.

The registers in a grocery store use code to know how much to charge.

Smart Speakers use code.

Coding helps with doing homework.

Cars are safer to drive because of code.

Texting uses code to send messages back and forth.

Smart toys use code to take commands and directions.

Coding can make cars that don't need a driver.

Coding controls traffic lights and traffic signs.

Coding is used to help control the temperature of your hot water.

Restaurants use code when taking reservations.

Machines that help doctors diagnose an illness use code.

Coding helps us have fresh vegetables all year long.

Lawyers use code to research laws that will help their clients.

Learning how to code is fun!

Athletes use code when exercising.

Coding helps when giving presentations.

Coding brings families closer together.

Designers use code to build and create furniture.

Architects use code when designing a new house.

Banks use coding to keep track of your money.

www.ingramcontent.com/pod-product-compliance
Lightning Source LLC
Chambersburg PA
CBHW081456060426
42444CB00037BA/3307